C000132266

FOR THE LOVE OF COFFEE

61 Things Every Coffee Lover Knows to Be True

TARA REED

SOURCEBOOKS, INC.®
NAPERVILLE, ILLINOIS

Published by Sourcebooks, Inc.
P.O. Box 4410, Naperville, Illinois 60567-4410
(630) 961-3900
Fax: (630) 961-2168
www.sourcebooks.com

ISBN-13: 978-1-4022-0886-7
ISBN-10: 1-4022-0886-3

Printed in China.
LEO   10   9   8   7   6   5   4   3   2   1

The best days to drink coffee are those that end in "Y".

SUNDAY

MONDAY

TUESDAY

WEDNESDAY

THURSDAY

FRIDAY

SATURDAY

Drink no coffee before its time.

How on earth do people live without coffee?

PABLO ESPRESSO

Steamy Night

Caffeine Attack

Mona Latté

9 coffees, 2006

Scream-out of coffee

There's no use crying over spilt coffee,
pour yourself some more.

Cup size matters.

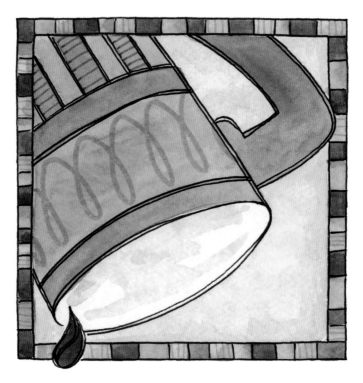

Without coffee, life just ain't worth livin'!

To caf or decaf, that is the question.

The best things in life are caffeinated.

Man cannot live by caffeine alone,
but he can give it his best shot!

The secret to a happy life is to
start each day with coffee.

Life is like coffee:
it's either hot or on the rocks.

I pour unto others,
as I would have others pour unto me.

Never put off till tomorrow
what you can drink today.

Imbibe while the coffee is hot.

I hear no decaf. I see no decaf.
I drink no decaf.

Life is what happens after drinking coffee.

Life is at its best when it's fully caffeinated.

Caffeine is the spice of life.

Life is too short to drink bad coffee.

Coffee: not just a drink, it's an adventure!

Cup of Coffee: $3.45
Caffeine Effect: Priceless!

Friends don't let friends drink decaf.

If you want coffee done right, brew it yourself.

If coffee is wrong, I don't want to be right.

Coffee is a gift I give myself.

Business before pleasure, but coffee before business.

Caffeinated we stand, decaffeinated we fall.

The end justifies the beans.

Coffee: never leave home without it.

Coffee is priority one!

Coffee conquers all.

Coffee: it's my reason for
getting out of bed in the morning.

I'm an equal opportunity drinker: espresso at breakfast, latté at lunch, and decaf at dinner.

Life is short. Drink coffee first.

Don't worry, drink coffee.

I always heed the call of caffeine.

Don't count your beans before they're brewed.

Call me crazy, but don't call me late for coffee.

Coffee is what separates us from the animals.

My best is always better after coffee.

January 1 - December 31
Peppy, shows zest for life
Sometimes slow to get started but then engergetic

I was born under the sign of coffee.

Coffee is the ultimate jackpot.

If at first you don't succeed, try another coffee.

I go from zero to sixty in just two sips!

Till I drank coffee, my life was incomplete.

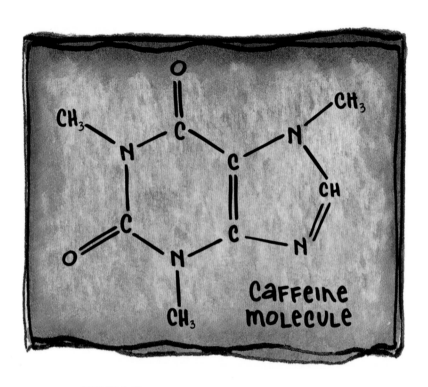

FINALLY, a reason to love chemistry!

2 oz. ESPRESSO
2 oz. TODDY COFFEE
2 TBLSP. chocolate SYRUP
1 tsp. sugar
DASH SKIM MILK
1 TBLSP. HAZELNUT SYRUP
WHIPPED CREAM
CHOCOLATE COVERED STRAWBERRY

Tara's Chocolate Coffee Delight

- BREW COFFEES, COMBINE.
- ADD SUGAR, MILK & FLAVORS.
- TOP WITH WHIPPED CREAM.
- GARNISH WITH STRAWBERRY.

enjoy!

To thine own brew be true.

One good cup deserves another.
(Repeat three times.)

Caffeine is the mother of invention.

What a coffee table is meant to be.

Time flies when you're having coffee.

Ultimately, it's all about the coffee.

Photo by Kyle Cowper

About the Author

Tara Reed creates fun and delightful collections for families and homes. After three years in creative design, she has twenty-three licenses under her belt including coasters, napkins, towels, mugs, and other items with such themes as holiday, seasonal, occasions, pets, coastal living, celebrations, and more. Tara lives in Portland, Oregon, with her son Kyle.

For more coffee love from Tara Reed,
visit www.coffeewit.com.